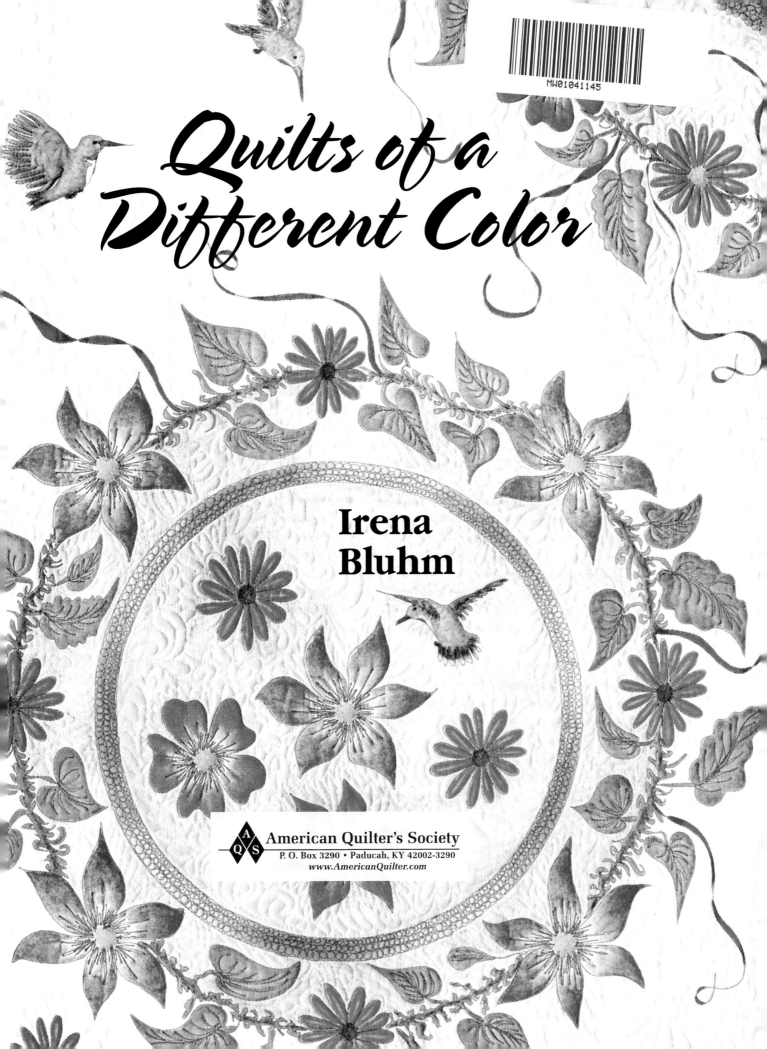

Quilts of a Different Color

Irena Bluhm

American Quilter's Society
P. O. Box 3290 • Paducah, KY 42002-3290
www.AmericanQuilter.com

Located in Paducah, Kentucky, the American Quilter's Society (AQS) is dedicated to promoting the accomplishments of today's quilters. Through its publications and events, AQS strives to honor today's quiltmakers and their work and to inspire future creativity and innovation in quiltmaking.

Text © 2008, Author, Irena Bluhm
Artwork © 2008, American Quilter's Society

EXECUTIVE EDITOR: NICOLE C. CHAMBERS
EDITOR: LINDA BAXTER LASCO
GRAPHIC DESIGN: ELAINE WILSON
COVER DESIGN: MICHAEL BUCKINGHAM
PHOTOGRAPHY: CHARLES R. LYNCH
HOW-TO PHOTOGRAPHY: IRENA BLUHM

American Quilter's Society
P. O. Box 3290 • Paducah, KY 42002-3290
www.AmericanQuilter.com

Additional copies of this book may be ordered from the American Quilter's Society, PO Box 3290, Paducah, KY 42002-3290, or online at www.AmericanQuilter.com.

Library of Congress Cataloging-in-Publication Data

Bluhm, Irena.
   Quilts of a different color / by Irena Bluhm.
      p. cm.
   ISBN 978-1-57432-955-1
1. Quilting. 2. Textile painting I. Title.

TT835.B51325 2008
746.46'041--dc22

2008011590

Proudly printed and bound in the United States of America

Dedication & Acknowledgments

Very special thanks go to

* two of my best quilting friends and teachers—Dr. Paula Peterson Platter and Linda V. Taylor—for rejoicing in everything I do and for being great role models and mentors. They are always there whenever I need some advice or support.

* my two daughters, Katharina Kompalka and Sylvia Golisano, for unconditional love, support, and always believing in me and my efforts.

* my husband, Richard, for having faith in me and for purchasing high quality equipment. Our lives have changed as a result.

Special thanks and appreciation to Gammill Quilting Systems for providing such a high-quality product. Very often she had to stand up to speeding ('way over 100 miles an hour!) from 8 to12 hours a day as I was racing with time to have the stitching finished as soon as I possibly could. We didn't get any speeding tickets, just some ribbons instead.

Becoming part of the quilting world opened my eyes to the compassion, friendship, and great support among quilters and all the people involved in this industry all over the country and abroad. I have met so many incredible people who reached out to me. Thank you for having faith in me. Thank you for embracing me. I am in great company, happy and proud to be a part of your world.

Contents

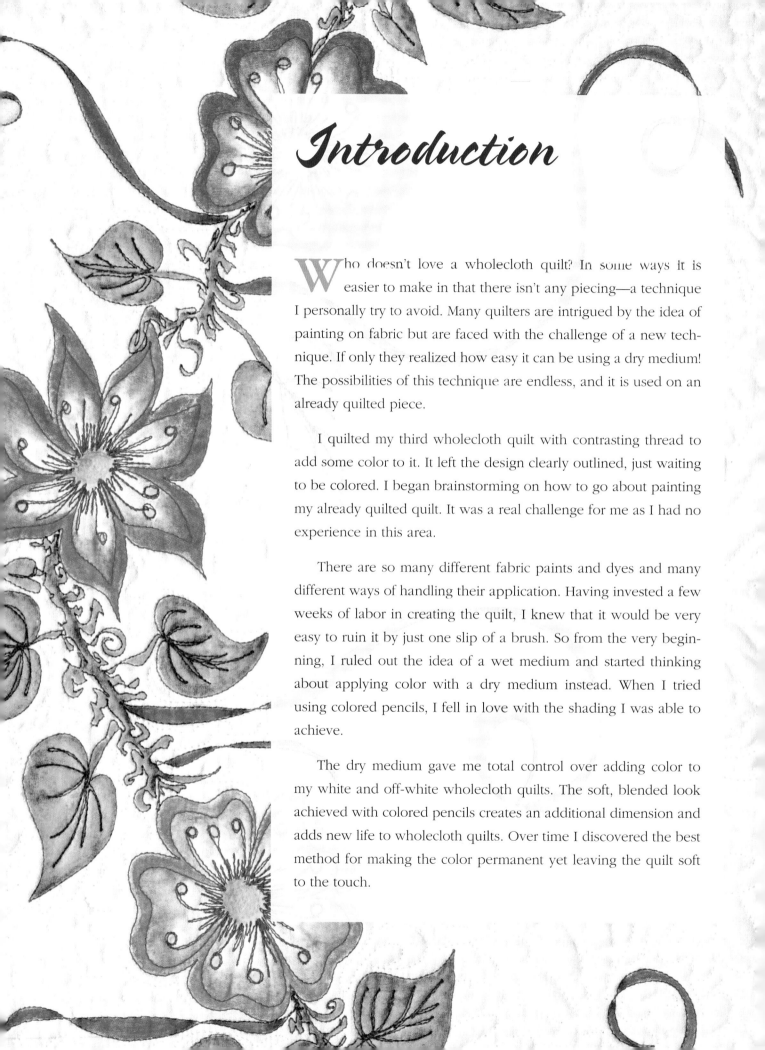

Introduction

Who doesn't love a wholecloth quilt? In some ways it is easier to make in that there isn't any piecing—a technique I personally try to avoid. Many quilters are intrigued by the idea of painting on fabric but are faced with the challenge of a new technique. If only they realized how easy it can be using a dry medium! The possibilities of this technique are endless, and it is used on an already quilted piece.

I quilted my third wholecloth quilt with contrasting thread to add some color to it. It left the design clearly outlined, just waiting to be colored. I began brainstorming on how to go about painting my already quilted quilt. It was a real challenge for me as I had no experience in this area.

There are so many different fabric paints and dyes and many different ways of handling their application. Having invested a few weeks of labor in creating the quilt, I knew that it would be very easy to ruin it by just one slip of a brush. So from the very beginning, I ruled out the idea of a wet medium and started thinking about applying color with a dry medium instead. When I tried using colored pencils, I fell in love with the shading I was able to achieve.

The dry medium gave me total control over adding color to my white and off-white wholecloth quilts. The soft, blended look achieved with colored pencils creates an additional dimension and adds new life to wholecloth quilts. Over time I discovered the best method for making the color permanent yet leaving the quilt soft to the touch.

Exposure to my work in the many venues where it has been shown has sparked a lot of interest in this technique. I've encountered more than a few amazed viewers at quilt shows asking how the quilts were done, who then shake their heads when I tell them. But once I explain the process, they start to think it might not be that difficult. It's not!

Since I started teaching, I've observed students in my class who are glued to their quilts, eager to finish so they can see the end result. They get very excited and enjoy the whole process in a very relaxed way as soon as they realize that it's not that difficult. It's time-consuming, but not difficult.

Anyone who can quilt a design motif—free-motion or with a stencil or pattern—should be able to add color to their own or their customers' quilts. It is a fun and innovative way to enhance any quilt that has first been quilted and that has a light background color. The quilt can include piecing, appliqué, trapunto, be whole-cloth, or of mixed techniques. As along as there are some blank spaces to fill in, you can add color to the quilting design motifs.

My painted-surface quilts are winning many awards in quilt contests nationwide. Some of my students have begun entering competitions with quilts they've made this way and their quilts are winning as well. So it's not just me. It's a great technique and one I'm eager to share.

Choosing a Theme

Before starting your quilt, ask yourself what kind of an effect you want to create. Light and airy? Full of color? Geometric? Organic? Then you can select quilting motifs that reflect your theme.

Don't worry about having the entire design mapped out in your head. After you have selected the quilting patterns, it is like a big puzzle. All you need to do is to fit the pieces together. Mark the layout of your design and decide on the placement of the elements. Then you can determine if you need to resize any patterns to fit your design.

The majority of my quilts were made marking only the perimeters of the motifs and then filling in the details with free-motion quilting as I went along. This may be an unconventional approach but is definitely more fun than marking every detail, and it has worked for me. I really don't see the "big picture" until the quilting is done. I like this because it makes me eager to finish the stitching and put the quilt up on the wall to see how it looks.

Choosing Your Materials

Quilt Supplies

Fabric

My favorite fabrics for this technique are:

* 100% cotton sateen
* 100% cotton, white or off-white, 90" wide Roc-lon®
  Ava-lon™ muslin, 200 thread count, bleached
* 100% cotton 108" wide Roc-lon® Dynasty™ Collection muslin

The pure white will provide better contrast as you color your quilt. Avoid rough textures, which make painting small details difficult. One-hundred percent unbleached cotton doesn't work well because of the cream color and some organic remnants within the fibers.

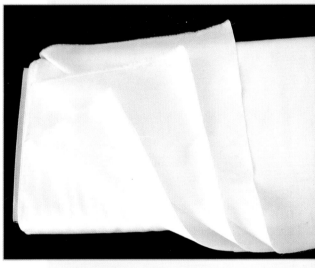

100% cotton sateen

I prefer using the same fabric on both the quilt top and back. Add at least 3" to the desired dimensions of your quilt top to account for shrinkage from quilting and washing. Make your batting and backing at least 4" larger than the quilt top (that is, 7" larger than the desired dimensions of the final quilt size). The extra 4" allowance gives you enough space to manipulate your quilt top during the quilting process.

Mark the main design elements using washable fabric markers. Never leave the marking lines on the fabric for an extended period of time. Removing them later can be difficult.

The sizing must be removed from the fabric before adding color. This can be done by prewashing before marking the quilt or when you soak the quilt after quilting to remove the quilting marks.

Preferred combo #1: Hobbs Heirloom® 100% bleached cotton on the bottom and Hobbs Cloud-Lite® low-loft resin-bonded polyester on top

Preferred combo #2: Hobbs Heirloom® cotton batting (80% cotton 20% polyester) on the bottom and Hobbs CloudLite® high-loft resin-bonded polyester on top

Batting

I use double batting to avoid problems with color bleeding to the back of the quilt. The textile medium applied to set the color can seep through a single layer of batting, taking some of the color with it. This problem is more likely if Jo Sonja's® Textile Medium is used by itself or if you are using polyester batting. If you use Delta Ceramcoat® Textile Medium or Versatex Fixer, you can use a single layer of any batting as long as it weighs at least 8 ounces.

Another advantage of using double batting is the faux trapunto effect that can be achieved. I usually use polyester batting on top and 100 percent bleached cotton batting on the bottom, the thicker the better. A heavier batting gives the quilt a better drape, in my opinion. The weight of the batting helps the quilt to hang flat. If you reverse the layering, the faux trapunto will have a firmer feel and will look flatter than when using polyester on the top layer.

Preferred combo #3: Quilters Dream Cotton Select on the bottom and Quilters Dream Poly on the top

Preferred combo #4: Quilters Dream Cotton Supreme on the bottom and Hobbs CloudLite® low-loft resin-bonded polyester on top

Thread

I recommend colored thread for the quilting to give you sharp lines outlining the areas to be colored. A high quality solid or variegated color works best. You're going to invest a lot of time in your project and you want to use the best possible materials.

Using a neutral, tone-on-tone thread for stitching the main design is easier to execute and works well with this technique. I prefer to use contrasting thread because I enjoy the challenge and the appearance of the end effect.

Coloring Supplies

You need very few basic supplies to get started with this technique:

colored pencils or oil paint sticks
textile medium
fixer
terry cloth towel
natural or synthetic bristle brushes
small plastic cup

Colored Pencils

Colored pencils are available at any store that sells art supplies. The only requirement is that they have thick, soft leads. Seven of my award-winning quilts were done with ordinary, readily available colored pencils.

There are many artist-grade brands of oil- or wax-based colored pencils and I used two of them on the wallhangings made for this book. Prisma-

Perma Core® and Maxi-Lock® thread of many different colors and YLI variegated thread have been used to stitch my quilts.

A basic starter kit is used in my classes.

Cautionary Tale

Never use any unbleached cotton batting with white, off white, or any light background fabric! Unbleached cotton or cotton/ polyester mix battings have cotton seed remnants that can cause hard to remove brown spots on your quilt.

Rose Art®, Crayola®, and Prang® pencils were used to color seven of my award-winning quilts.

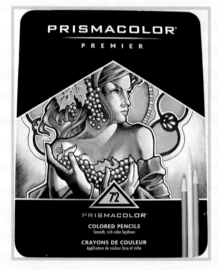

High-quality colored pencils. Some art stores have open stock.

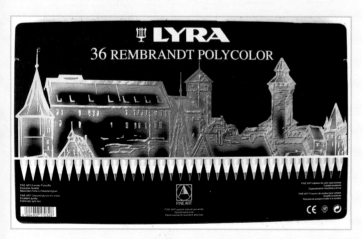

High-quality oil-based colored pencils

color® Premier Colored Pencils have thick soft leads made from light-resistant pigments. The colors are easily blended, slow to wear, and waterproof. They are sold in different-size packages up to 120 colors. The colors take on a deeper tone after the textile-medium application. If you like soft pastel colors, you should go easy by not pressing too hard during the color application.

It is best to test the colors on a piece of the same fabric you'll be using in your quilt. When you are satisfied with the color, apply the textile medium and check the effect. The values may change to a darker tone. I noticed this when using the Prismacolor pencils.

The oil-based Lyra Rembrandt Polycolor pencils worked just as beautifully. They are rich in pigment and easy to apply.

I like to buy open stock pencils. On average, it takes me 5–9 pencils of each color to make one quilt. Open stock ensures that I can match the colors when I need to buy more.

I also recommend Prismacolor® Scholar® Colored Pencils, Faber-Castell Polychromos Artists' Color Pencils, and Caran D'Ache Pablo® Colored Pencils.

Read all the descriptions of any product before you decide which one to buy. You can also buy large boxes of colored pencils at a discount price at teacher supply stores. They're great if you are going to be doing lots of quilts or if you decide to teach this technique, something I'd love to see happen.

Paint Sticks

A color option I've tried with success is oil-based paint sticks. Shiva® Artist's Paintstik® oil paints come in regular and iridescent colors.

I use a shorter and firmer bristle brush than I do for applying textile medium. These are made of hog hair. Any firm brush or a stencil brush will do.

The three brushes at the bottom were used to color STARBURST.

BELOW: *STARBURST in progress. The three bottom brushes in the photo to the right were used.*

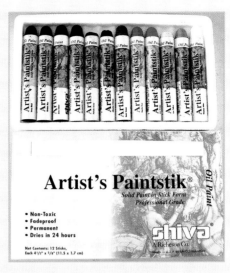

Shiva® Artists Paintstik® oil-based paint sticks

Firm bristle brushes made of hog hair

Apply a base coat of one color then layer a darker color for the shading.

Use a towel or cloth to protect from falling particles from the paint stick.

BELOW: *Oil paint stick color application is very smooth and easy to blend. Delta Ceramcoat was used to seal the color application on this quilt.*

I used a separate brush for each color while working on the quilt. That way, I could avoid cleaning the brushes before moving on to apply a different color.

You can apply a base coat of one color, then layer on a different color, usually darker, for the shading.

When not in use, the paint sticks will self seal, forming a film over the working end. Before each use, you need to peel off the film. Use caution and do that away from your quilt. During color application, hold the paint stick in your non-dominant hand over a towel while you load your stencil brush with the color. This will protect your quilt from any little particles of paint that may try to find their way onto the background.

Oil paint stick color application is very smooth and you can easily blend the colors.

Use mineral spirits to clean your brushes or work them onto a wet bar of soap. With either method, rinse with soap and water then dry the brushes before using them again.

Clean your brushes before you take a break. When you resume, your brushes will be ready to use. Do not let your brushes sit for a long time with paint on them. The paint will dry and become harder to remove.

Textile Medium and Fixer

Jo Sonja's Textile Medium is the consistency of liquid soap and is what makes the color permanent. It is available from Blick Art Materials (see Resources, pages 92–93). If used by itself or with polyester batting, it is more likely to seep through your quilt. Using double batting prevents bleeding through to the back of the quilt.

I also use Delta Ceramcoat Textile Medium with great success. It is the most user-friendly product because of its consistency. It is available at craft supply chain stores nationwide.

To make the textile medium even thicker, I add Versatex Fixer. It is a no-heat fixer and eliminates the need for heat-setting the color. It is available from Dharma Trading Company (see Resources, pages 92–93).

Terry Cloth Towel

As I'm working on coloring a quilt, I keep all the pencils I need on top of a terrycloth towel, which I lay on top of my quilt. The pencils are right where I need them and the towel protects the quilt from any accidental coloring.

Natural Bristle Brushes

Natural bristle brushes are the best choice for applying textile medium. They hold more of the textile medium as they are more absorbent than synthetic brushes. Brush sets with several different sizes can be purchased at any store that sells art supplies.

Plastic Cup

I like to pour out only small amounts of textile medium at a time so I can apply it all before it dries out. A one-ounce plastic cup, the kind that comes with cold medicines, is perfect.

Textile medium and fixer

One-ounce plastic cup

Cautionary Tale

You must apply textile medium of your choice over the oil paint stick application! Heat setting does not work! The areas will smear or rub off even after months of drying time. Heat setting just makes the paint application dry to the touch. That's all!

Additional Advice

When you use paint sticks for color application, you can also use colored pencils for small detail work whenever the paint stick application becomes too difficult on small details. I strongly recommend Lyra Rembrandt oil-based colored pencils for use with oil paint sticks wherever needed.

Marking and Quilting Your Quilt Top

Preparing a Master Pattern

Start with a plain piece of paper the size of your project.

Fold the paper in half diagonally, then fold in half and in half again, creating 8 triangular segments.

Make reference lines by drawing along the fold lines with a Sharpie® permanent marker and a straight-edge ruler.

Draw your quilting motifs on the pattern, using the reference lines to space their placement, placing the design motif over a light box, then placing the paper over the motif and tracing it onto the master pattern. Assuming a symmetrical design, you only need to draw an eighth, quarter, or half of the design, depending on the repeat, then refold the pattern paper and trace the design on the other portions of the pattern.

Marking the Quilt Top

Cut a square of fabric to the size of your project, adding at least 3" to allow for shrinkage from quilting and washing. Make sure it is squared off perfectly.

Fold the quilt top in half diagonally as shown, and press along the fold line.

Fold in half again and press along the fold line.

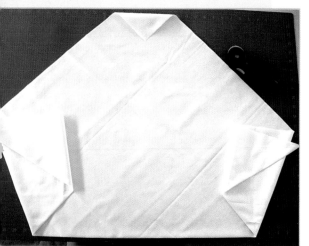

Fold fabric in half diagonally.

Quilts of a Different Color ✳ Irena Bluhm

Open the second fold, then bring the folded edges in toward the first fold line as shown and press along the fold lines.

By unfolding those last two folds, you can see the pressed reference lines that will match the reference lines on your pattern.

Open out your square of fabric and trace along the fold lines with a blue washable marking pen and a straight edge ruler.

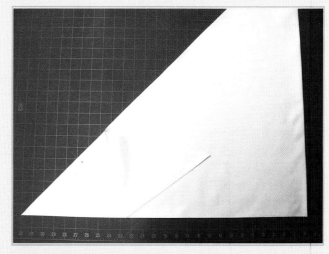

Fold in half again and press.

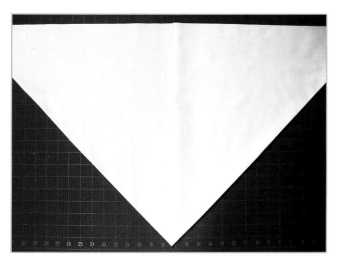

Open the second fold, bring folded edges toward the first fold, and press.

Draw reference lines on fold lines for pattern placement.

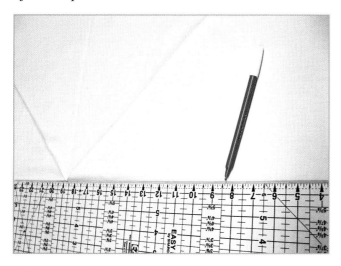

Trace along the folded lines with a blue washable pen.

Lines are marked.

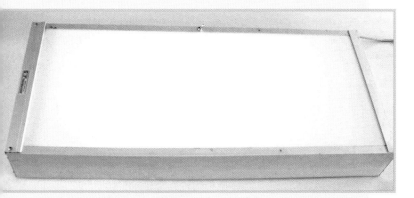

X-ray viewer or light box

Trace the center of your design first. Lay your pattern on a light or glass or Plexiglas® sheet with a light beneath. I use an X-ray viewer.

Secure the pattern with tape.

Lay the quilt top fabric over the pattern, using the reference marks to line up the fabric with the pattern.

Pin the fabric to the pattern.

Use washable marking pens to trace the design onto the fabric.

Continue to trace the pattern motifs, using the reference lines to ensure proper placement on the quilt.

Make sure you leave a 3" margin from the edge of the design to the edge of your quilt top.

There are two ways of tracing or transferring the design onto the fabric:

Pin the fabric to the pattern.

Washable marking pens

Be sure to leave a 3" margin from the edge.

Quilts of a Different Color ✴ Irena Bluhm

METHOD #1

Create a paper master pattern the size of the quilt as described above.

Pin the quilt top onto the paper master pattern and place it on top of a light box. Trace the design onto the fabric over the light box.

METHOD #2

Mark all reference lines directly on the quilt top as described above.

Place a pattern used for the center on top of the light box and secure it using Scotch® tape.

Place your quilt top over the pattern and line it up with the reference lines for the perfect design placement in the center. You can remove the scotch tape at this point and trace the design after you pin the quilt to the pattern below.

Place a corner or a border motif on top of the light box and secure it. Place your quilt top over, line it up using reference lines for the design placement, and pin it together.

Once you have a complete repeat of the design marked, transfer the design to the other parts by folding the quilt top accordingly and using the light box.

When I do my marking, I simply outline the shape of many of the motifs, often using a compass.

The details are filled in with free-motion quilting.

RIGHT: *Outline design and marked fill-in design areas*

Cautionary Tale

This quilt was marked with a dry, washable pink/magenta marking pencil and stored in a non-air-conditioned room for a few months. The lines turned yellow and I had an extremely hard time washing them out. I had used this marker before but had always washed out the lines within three weeks with no problem.

The entire design motif can be marked on the quilt top.

Alternatively, the entire design motif can be marked on the quilt top.

Following the marked lines accurately takes some practice. However, straying off the lines is not a worry (as long as your stitching lines are smooth and not wobbly) because that will never show after the marked lines are washed out.

I quilt all the design motifs first.

After all the main design motifs are done, I do the background stitching, enhancing the faux trapunto effect. I stitch around all the design motifs first and fill in the rest as I go.

Design motifs are quilted first.

RIGHT: *After the main designs are done background stitching is added.*

Quilts of a Different Color ✳ Irena Bluhm

Preparing Your Quilt for Coloring

After all of the quilting is finished, soak your quilt in a bathtub filled with cold water to remove all markings. This will also remove any sizing if you did not prewash your fabric. I usually leave the quilt soaking for 30 minutes to an hour.

Carefully remove the quilt, draping it over your arm as the water drains off. Run it through a spin cycle in your washing machine if you wish or simply let the water drain out. Lay the quilt flat to dry, or hang it to dry and use a steamer to flatten it after it is dry. It is an absolute "must" that your quilt be flat before you start coloring.

At this point, you can square up, trim, and bind your quilt, but don't add a sleeve as it will interfere with the coloring process. Most of the time, I apply the binding after the coloring process is complete because I prefer to use the colors on the quilt to determine the color for the binding.

Here is how CHERISH FLOWERS AND RIBBONS looked before the color was applied.

Using Colored Pencils

Shading is controlled by the amount of pressure you apply.

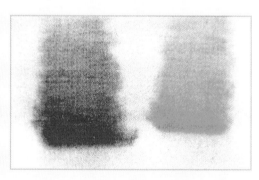

Use caution to avoid smudges and prevent color transfer.

Shading is controlled by applying more or less pressure. In this example, I started with a lot of pressure and gradually applied less and less, blending the color with the light background. The very dark color "burnishing" is achieved by applying plenty of pressure.

Although colored pencils are a dry medium, you still need to be cautious about touching, rubbing, or disturbing the already-colored areas to prevent color transfer to the background. You need to protect all the colored areas until a textile medium is applied and has dried completely.

I purposely created a smudge to show you what can happen if you don't use caution. The darker color can spread to an area you want to remain uncolored.

Often, a smudge is simply loose pigment that is sitting on the surface of the quilt. The solution is to seal the adjacent design motif by applying textile medium and then blowing or shaking the loose pigment off the quilt. Most of the time, that's all it takes.

If the pigment has settled into the fabric, the deeper smudge can be removed with a Clorox® Bleach® Pen or Tide-to-Go® stain remover.

Read all the instructions that come with these products before using them on your quilt. Make sure all surrounding areas with color have been set with textile medium. Then use these products sparingly. If you apply too much and drench an area, color may seep to the back of the quilt.

The Clorox pen has a wider tip and is good for larger areas. It is very potent, so don't leave it on for a long time. Rinse the area thoroughly once the stain has disappeared.

Tide-to-Go stain remover is milder and good on smaller areas. I used it on a small spot on a show quilt recently, and leaving it on without rinsing did not cause a problem.

Take your time and enjoy the coloring process. It can be fun and relaxing if you're not rushed.

The Clorox Bleach Pen has a wider tip and is good for larger areas.

The Tide-to-Go pen is milder and good for smaller areas.

Applying the Color

Tips for Success

As you are applying color, work from left to right if you are right-handed and from right to left if you are left-handed. This will keep your hand from having to rest on top of the colored areas.

Keep your quilt perfectly flat, lying on top of a large table, ideally with access from all four sides.

Wear clean clothes with sleeves over your elbows to prevent oil stains.

Keep the pencils for a quilt separate from your other pencils.

Note which brands and colors you use for each of your design motifs. Colors are different from brand to brand, even if they happen to have the same name. It is very easy to forget which colors you used (believe me!), especially if you take long breaks during the process.

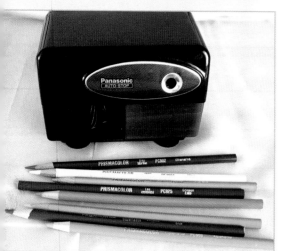

Use an electric pencil sharpener often, being careful not to get your points too sharp.

Use an electric pencil sharpener and use it frequently. You'll have less breakage and waste. Be careful not to make the points too sharp. A needle-sharp point can damage your fabric.

Start in the middle of your quilt and work toward the edges, protecting the uncolored areas from any accidents by covering them with a towel or piece of fabric. Note, however, that a towel should not be used over colored but untreated areas.

Use pictures of flowers, leaves, or other objects in your design as a reference for coloring and shading.

Use pictures of flowers, leaves, or other objects that appear in your design motifs as a reference to help you with choosing your colors and shading.

To achieve shading, use several values of the same color or vary the pressure (and therefore the amount of color applied) as you apply the colors. Placing the darkest values at the edges and shading with lighter values in the center creates a highlighted effect.

I started this leaf with red and yellow lightly applied in the center.

I continued adding different shades of green. On the cherry, I applied red around the edges first. Notice the darker tone toward the bottom. This gives a 3-D effect.

I added yellow on top of the other layers of color on both the cherry and leaf. It makes the colors more lively.

Careful placement of highlights will make an implied light source consistent.

This leaf was started with red and yellow lightly applied in the center.

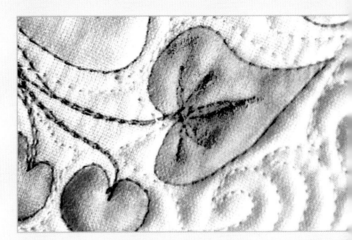

Different shades of green were added on the leaf. The cherry has red applied around the edges first, with darker tone giving a 3-D effect.

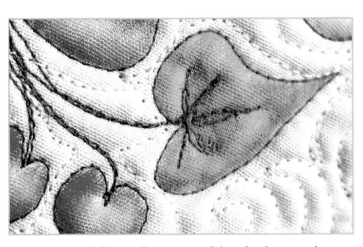

Adding yellow on top of the other layers makes them more lively.

RIGHT: *Careful placement of highlights makes an implied light source consistent.*

Pencils can collect lint from the quilt as you are coloring with them. Clean off any accumulated lint before using them again.

Use good lighting.

Keep the quilt away from direct sunlight.

Color one portion of a design motif at a time—one petal, one section of a feather, and so on.

When a colored area is finished, it's time for the next step—application of the textile medium.

Apply the textile medium before you take a break or finish for the day. When you do take a break, be sure to mark the last design motif where the textile medium was applied so you will know exactly where to continue when you return.

Color one portion of the design motif at a time.

When a colored area is finished it is time to apply the textile medium.

Things to Avoid

Never rest the palm of your hand or an elbow on top of the colored areas before you have applied textile medium.

Never fold the quilt in any way while trying to put it up on a wall or to move or otherwise manipulate it. No matter how careful you are, sooner or later you will transfer pigment from the colored areas onto the background. (Don't ask me how I know!)

Never leave the colored areas exposed and unprotected by application of textile medium.

Applying Textile Medium

Although each can be used separately, I prefer a mixture of these three products to make the applied color permanent. I start with the Delta Ceramcoat Textile Medium, pour the Versatex Fixer on top, then add the Jo Sonja's medium and mix. I use the following proportions:

70% Jo Sonja's Textile Medium
20% Delta Ceramcoat Textile Medium
10% Versatex Fixer

All three products are water-based and non-toxic. Versatex Fixer is the only one that doesn't require heat setting, but if it's mixed with the others, the mixture can be used without heat setting.

Mix a small amount and fill a small plastic cup with about a tablespoon or more of the mixture. Keep the rest in a covered jar or in the original container.

Use a natural bristle brush to apply the mixture, choosing a size depending on the size of the motifs you are coating. I use a soft watercolor liner for the very small details, a ¼" watercolor shader for the smaller motifs, and a ⅝" brush for the larger ones.

Use a small plastic cup to hold the mixture and apply it as you would paint.

Keep your brush slanted away from the edge and toward the center.

Try to avoid drenching the holes made by the needle during the quilting, especially if you are using Jo Sonja's textile medium by itself. This will minimize the risk of the medium seeping through to the back.

Start with Delta Ceramcoat Textile Medium and Versatex Fixer.

Add Jo Sonja's Textile Medium, then mix.

Rest only your wrist directly on the quilt, with your palm off and above the colored areas.

Apply the mixture to one color at a time and rinse the brush with water between colors.

Avoid overloading your brush with the textile medium.

Apply the textile medium sparingly to avoid drenching the treated areas. You just need to make sure the area is completely covered by the medium.

Rinse the cup and brush with water every time you run out of the mixture.

Rest only your wrist directly on the quilt. Avoid overloading your brush with the textile medium, and apply sparingly.

Things to Avoid

Don't leave your textile medium mixture open to the air. It will dry out, develop clumps, and become rubbery, making application difficult.

Keep food and beverages at a distance.

Don't allow a fan to blow onto your work. It can lift up some of the pigment from the colored areas, allowing it to settle elsewhere on your quilt.

Don't ever dilute the textile medium or fixer with water. It increases the chances of color seeping to the back of your quilt.

Caring For Your Quilt

My quilts rarely get washed, but when they do, I like to wash them by hand with no soaking, using quilt soap or a mild detergent. Some quilters have reported success with washing their colored quilts in the machine. The only color that suffered was on areas where the textile medium wasn't applied.

Projects

In each of the following projects, you'll find a photograph of the finished quilt, the materials you need, the quilting motifs, the enlargement percentages to duplicate the size of the original project, a placement diagram showing where the motifs should be traced onto the fabric, and color guidance.

Refer to pages 9–28 for batting selection, quilting advice, and color-application instructions. Remember, you do not need to use the colored pencil brands specified. Use them as a guide to select colors from the brand of your choice.

Choose your favorite method for binding your finished quilt. You'll need additional fabric for the binding.

Cherish Flowers and Ribbons

27" x 27" ✳ *quilted and colored by the author*

Cherish Flowers and Ribbons

27" x 27"

Materials

⅞ yard background fabric

1 yard backing

Batting 34" x 34"

Rose Art colored pencils:

Purple, Violet, Pink, Cherry Red, Red, Golden Yellow, Burgundy, Light Green, Grass Green, and True Green

Color Placement

FLOWERS: Purple, Violet, Pink, Cherry Red, Red, Golden Yellow, and Burgundy

LEAVES: Light Green, Grass Green, True Green, Red, Golden Yellow

RIBBONS, CHERRIES, AND CENTER: Golden Yellow, Cherry Red, and Burgundy

BACKGROUND: Golden Yellow, Red, Light Green, and Purple

Sewing Instructions

Cut a square of background fabric 30" x 30".

Enlarge the quilting motif and trace it onto the center of the background fabric.

Layer the top with batting and backing and quilt the motifs and background fill.

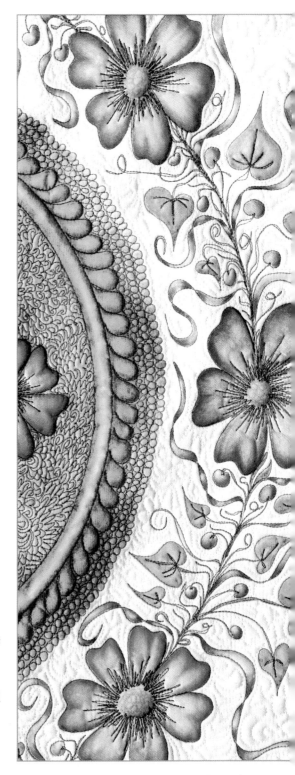

After finishing the quilting, remove the traced lines according to the manufacturer's instructions.

If you did not prewash your fabric, soak the quilt to remove the sizing.

After the quilt is dry, flatten it by blocking or steaming.

Apply and set the color (review the instructions on pages 21–28).

Trim the finished quilt to measure 27" x 27".

Use your favorite method to bind the raw edges. ✴

placement diagram

Cherish Flowers and Ribbons

Cherish Flowers and Ribbons–1

Enlarge pattern 200%

Cherish Flowers and Ribbons–2

Enlarge pattern 200%

2

Cherish Flowers and Ribbons

Cherish Flowers and Ribbons–3

Enlarge pattern 200%

③

Cherish Flowers and Ribbons–4

Enlarge pattern 200%

Fly Away

12½" x 12½" ✳ by Carla Scott of Quilted Frog, McKinney, Texas

Fly Away

19½" x 19½"

Materials

1 fat quarter background fabric
⅝ yard backing
Batting 19½" x 19½"
Prismacolor Pencils:
Electric Blue, Light Green, Process Red, Neon Pink, Violet, Grass Green, Yellowed Orange, Chartreuse, Apple Green, Vert Printemps, Non-Photo Blue, Electric Blue, Blue Vert Pale

Color Placement

BUTTERFLY: Electric Blue, Light Green, Process Red, and Neon Pink

FLOWER: Violet, Neon Pink, and Process Red

LEAVES: Grass Green, Yellowed Orange, Chartreuse, Apple Green, and Vert Printemps

RIBBON: Non-Photo Blue, Electric Blue, and Blue Vert Pale

Sewing Instructions

Cut a square of background fabric 15½" x 15½".

Enlarge the quilting motif and trace it onto the center of the background fabric.

Layer the top with batting and backing and quilt the motifs and background fill.

After finishing the quilting, remove the traced lines according to the manufacturer's instructions.

If you did not prewash your fabric, soak the quilt to remove the sizing.

After the quilt is dry, flatten it by blocking or steaming.

Apply and set the color (review the instructions on pages 21–28).

Trim the finished quilt to a circle 12½" in diameter.

Use your favorite method to bind the raw edges. ✳

Fly Away

placement diagram

Pattern shown at 100%

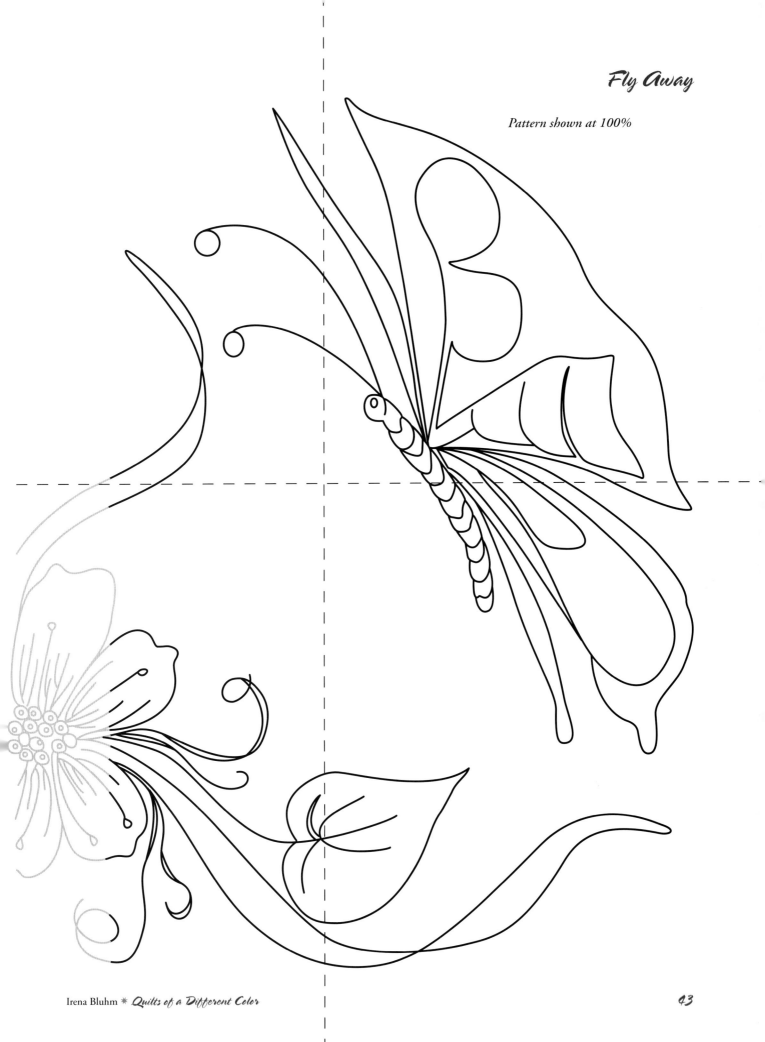

Dragonflies

19" x 19" ✳ *quilted and colored by the author*

Dragonflies

19" x 19"

Materials

¾ yard background fabric

¾ yard backing

Batting 26" x 26"

⅝ yard for back of pillow

18" x 18" pillow form

Lyra Rembrandt Colored Pencils:

Viridian, True Blue, Light Carmine, Canary Yellow,
Van Dyke Brown

Color Placement

SPIDER'S WEB: Viridian

DRAGONFLY WINGS: True Blue, Canary Yellow, and
Light Carmine

DRAGONFLY BODIES: Van Dyke Brown

Sewing Instructions

Cut a square of background fabric 22" x 22".

Enlarge the quilting motif and trace it onto the center of the
background fabric.

Layer the top with batting and backing and quilt the motifs and
background fill.

Hem by folding under ¼" and then 1", stitching by machine.

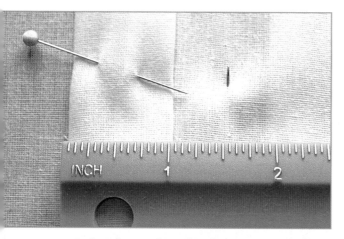

Right sides together, align the raw edges with hemmed edges in toward the center of the pillow, creating a 3" overlap.

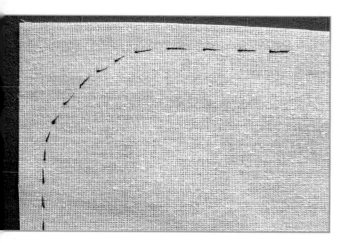

Mark rounded corners as shown.

After finishing the quilting, remove the traced lines according to the manufacturer's instructions.

If you did not prewash your fabric, soak the pillow top to remove the sizing.

After the pillow top is dry, flatten it by blocking or steaming.

Apply and set the color (review the instructions on pages 21–28).

Trim the finished pillow top to measure 19½" x 19½".

Cut two pieces 19½" x 12½" of the pillow back fabric.

Hem along a 19½" side of both pieces by folding under ¼" and then 1". Stitch by machine.

Place the hemmed pieces right sides together on the right side of the finished pillow top, aligning the raw edges, with the hemmed edges in toward the center of the pillow, creating a 3" overlap.

Mark rounded corners as shown.

Sew completely around the pillow edges with a ¼" seam allowance.

Clip the curved corners. Turn right-side out and insert the pillow form. ✳

placement diagram

Pattern shown at 100%

Rotate 60° to make the full design.

From Heart 2 Heart

34" x 34" ✳ *quilted and colored by the author*

From Heart 2 Heart

34" x 34"

Materials

1⅛ yards background fabric

1¼ yards backing

Batting 41" x 41"

Rose Art Colored Pencils:

Magenta, Cardinal Red, Purple, Violet, Burgundy, Blush Pink, Cerise, Light Green, Pine Green, Golden Yellow

Color Placement

FEATHERS, POM-POMS, AND RIBBONS: Magenta, Cardinal Red, Purple, Violet, and Burgundy

HEARTS: Blush Pink and Cerise

LEAVES: Light Green, Pine Green, Cardinal Red, and Golden Yellow

Sewing Instructions

Cut a square of background fabric 37" x 37".

Enlarge the quilting motifs and trace them onto the background fabric according to the placement diagram.

Layer the top with batting and backing and quilt the motifs and background fill.

After finishing the quilting, remove the traced lines according to the manufacturer's instructions.

If you did not prewash your fabric, soak the quilt to remove the sizing.

After the quilt is dry, flatten it by blocking or steaming.

Apply and set the color (review the instructions on pages 21–28).

Trim the finished quilt to measure 34" x 34".

Use your favorite method to bind the raw edges. ✳

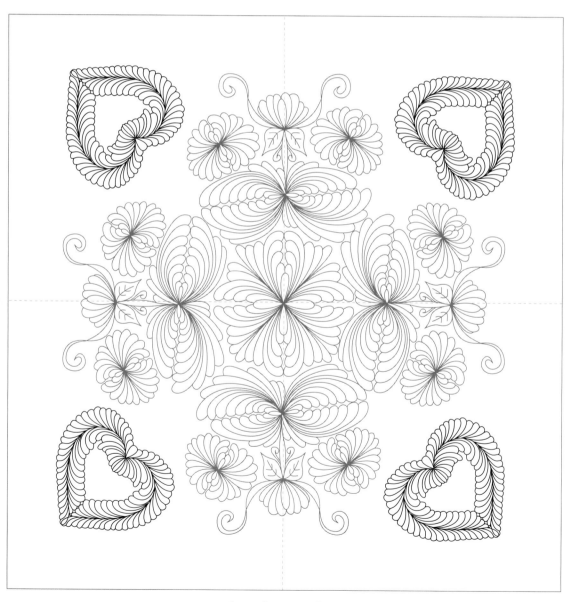

quilting placement diagram

Feathered Heart

Pattern shown at 100%

From Heart 2 Heart

Featherbuds

Enlarge pattern 200%

Rotate 90° to make the full design.

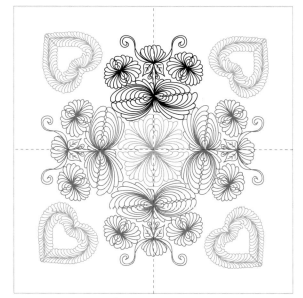

placement diagram

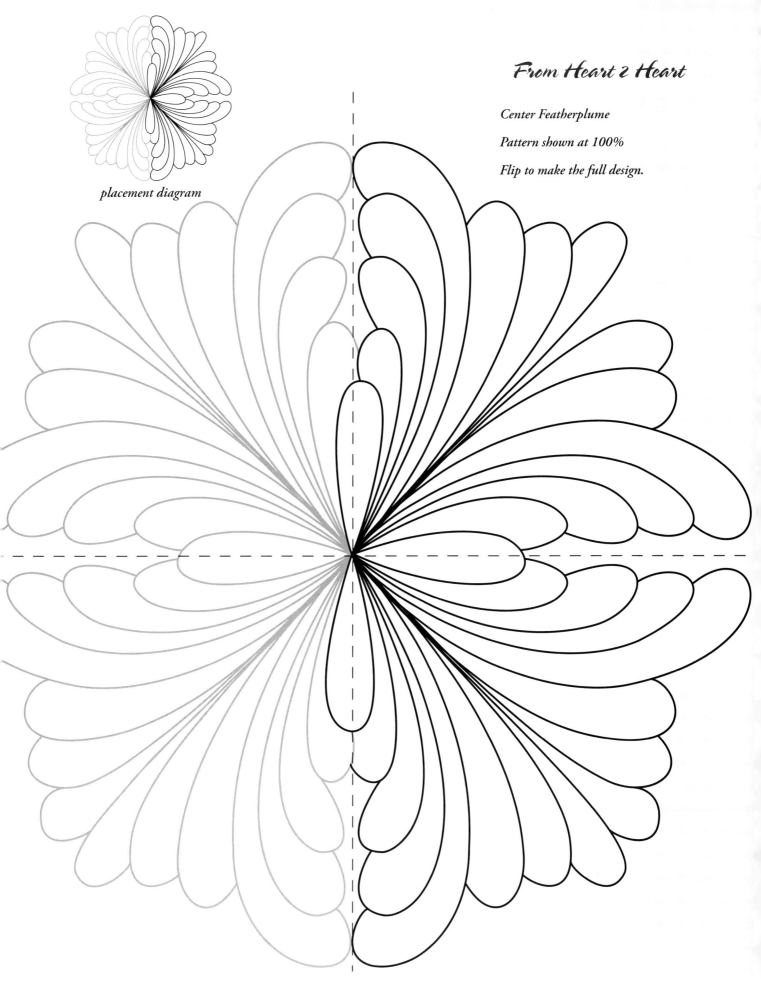

Center Featherplume

Pattern shown at 100%

Flip to make the full design.

placement diagram

Featherlight

38" x 38" ✳ quilted and colored by the author

Featherlight

38" x 38"

Materials

1¼ yards background fabric

1⅜ yards backing

Batting 45" x 45"

Lyra Rembrandt Colored Pencils:

Light Blue, Dark Orange, Canary Yellow, Apple Green, Viridian

Color Placement

INNER CENTER PLUMES: Light Blue

OUTER CENTER PLUMES: Viridian

CORNER PLUMES: Light Blue and Viridian

OUTER EDGE PLUMES: Apple Green

HIGHLIGHTING: Canary Yellow

Sewing Instructions

Cut a square of background fabric 41" x 41".

Enlarge the quilting motifs and trace them onto the background fabric according to the placement diagram.

Layer the top with batting and backing and quilt the motifs and background fill.

After finishing the quilting, remove the traced lines according to the manufacturer's instructions.

If you did not prewash your fabric, soak the quilt to remove the sizing.

After the quilt is dry, flatten it by blocking or steaming.

Apply and set the color (review the instructions on pages 21–28).

Trim the finished quilt to measure 38" x 38". ✳

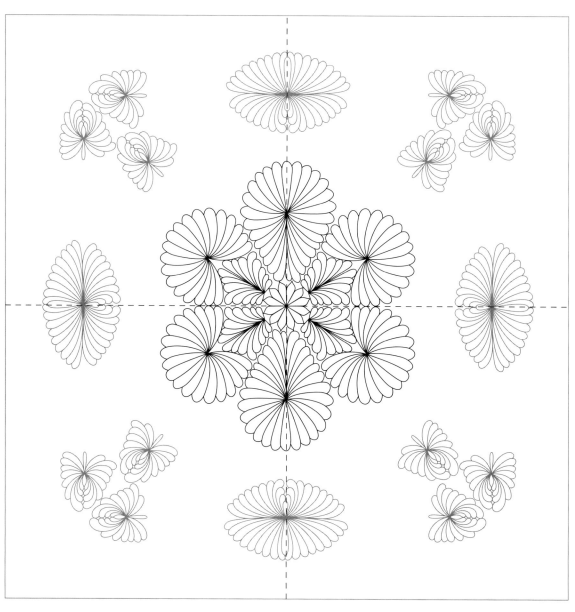

quilting placement diagram

Center Featherplumes

Enlarge pattern 250%

Featherlight

Outer Pom-Pom

Pattern shown at 100%

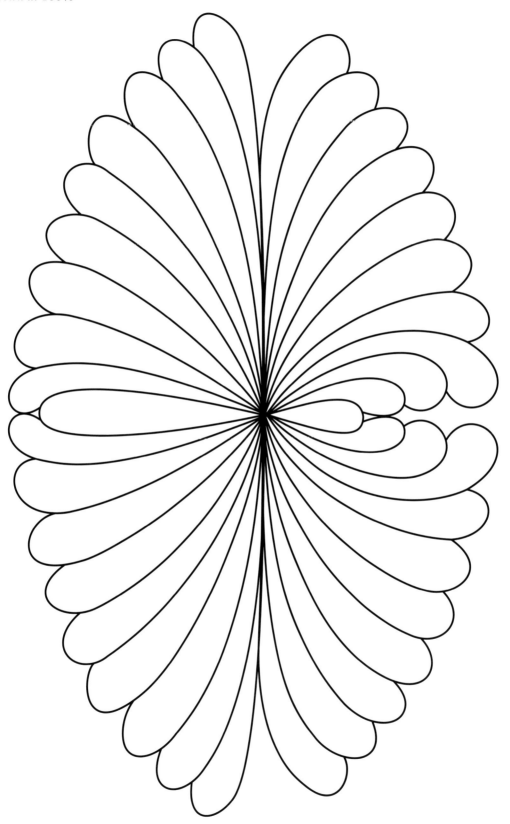

Corner Featherplumes

Pattern shown at 100%

placement diagram

Horseshoe

27" x 27" ✳ quilted and colored by the author

Horseshoe

27" x 27"

Materials

⅞ yard background fabric

1 yard backing

Batting 34" x 34"

Rose Art Colored Pencils:
   Peacock Green, Green

Color Placement

Fill with Peacock Green and accent with the Green.

Sewing Instructions

Cut a square of background fabric 30" x 30".

Enlarge the quilting motifs and trace them onto the background fabric according to the placement diagram.

Layer the top with batting and backing and quilt the motifs and background fill.

After finishing the quilting, remove the traced lines according the manufacturer's instructions.

If you did not prewash your fabric, soak the quilt to remove the sizing.

After the quilt is dry, flatten it by blocking or steaming.

Apply and set the color (review the instructions on pages 21–28).

Trim the finished quilt to measure 27" x 27".

Use your favorite method to bind the raw edges. ✳

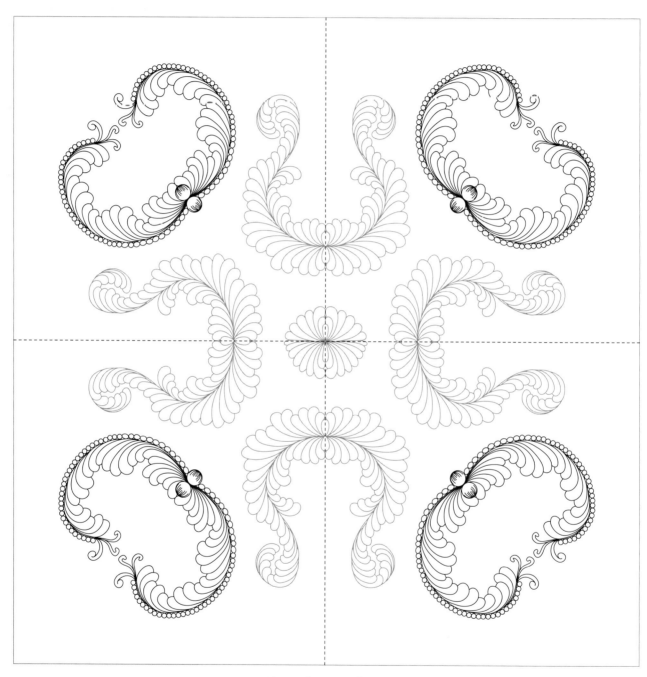

quilting placement diagram

Outer Featherplume

Pattern shown at 100%

Horseshoe

Center Pom-Pom

Pattern shown at 100%

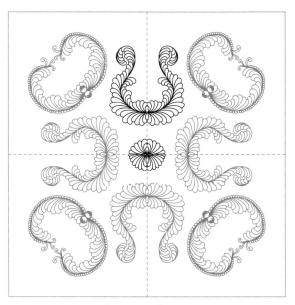

placement diagram

Inner Featherplume

Pattern shown at 100%

Flowerburst

19" x 19" ✻ quilted and colored by the author

Flowerburst

19" x 19"

Materials

¾ yard background fabric

¾ yard backing

Batting 26" x 26"

⅝ yard for back of pillow

18" x 18" pillow form

Colored Pencils:

Moss Green, Apple Green, Geranium Lake, Vermillion,
Canary Yellow, Violet

Color Placement

CENTER FLOWER: Violet

STAR: Moss Green

STAR BACKGROUND: Canary Yellow

OUTER PETALS: Vermillion

OUTER BUDS: Apple Green

Sewing Instructions

Cut a square of background fabric 22" x 22".

Enlarge the quilting motif and trace it onto the center of the
background fabric.

Layer the top with batting and backing and quilt the motifs and background fill.

After finishing the quilting, remove the traced lines according to the manufacturer's instructions.

If you did not prewash your fabric, soak the pillow top to remove the sizing.

After the pillow top is dry, flatten it by blocking or steaming.

Apply and set the color (review the instructions on pages 21–28).

Trim the finished pillow top to measure 19½" x 19½".

Finish the pillow according to the instructions on page 46. ✳

placement diagram

Flowerburst motif

Pattern shown at 100%

Rotate pattern 45° to complete the design

Plumes of Feathers

47" x 48" ✳ quilted and colored by the author

Plumes of Feathers

47" x 48"

Materials

1½ yards background fabric (54" wide)

1⅝ yards backing

Batting 54" x 55"

Lyra Rembrandt Colored Pencils

Moss Green, Apple Green, Ochre, Pale Geranium Lake, Dark Carmine

Color Placement

Center motif: All colors listed; refer to quilt photo

Inner border feathers and pom-poms: Dark Carmine and Pale Geranium Lake

Outer border feathers and pom-poms: Apple Green and Ochre

Sewing Instructions

Cut a square of background fabric 50" x 51".

Enlarge the quilting motifs and trace them onto the background fabric according to the placement diagram.

Layer the top with batting and backing and quilt the motifs and background fill.

After finishing the quilting, remove the traced lines according to the manufacturer's instructions.

If you did not prewash your fabric, soak the quilt to remove the sizing.

After the quilt is dry, flatten it by blocking or steaming.

Apply and set the color (review the instructions on pages 21–28).

Trim the finished quilt to measure 47" x 48".

Use your favorite method to bind the raw edges. ✳

placement diagram

Center motif

Enlarge pattern 250%

Plumes of Feathers

Border Pom-Pom

Pattern shown at 100%

placement diagram

Center Border Featherplume

Pattern shown at 100%

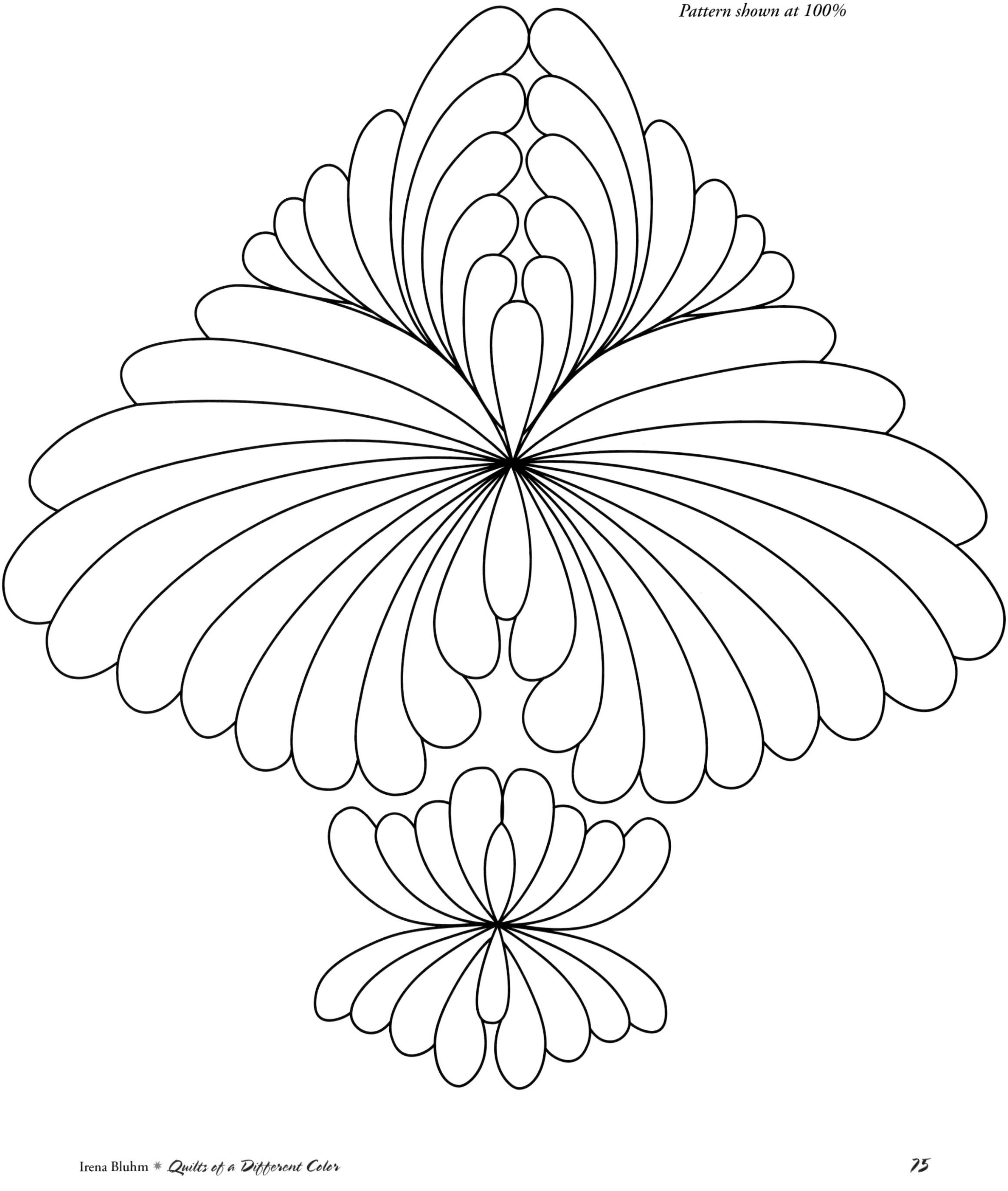

Border Featherplume

Enlarge pattern 200%

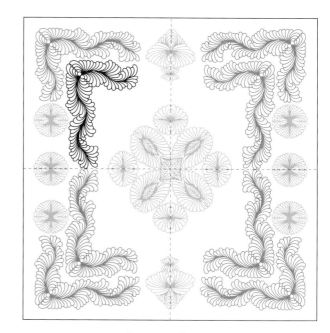

placement diagram

Gallery of Quilts

Paula's Star Generator

39" x 37" ✳ pieced by Paula Peterson Platter; quilted, colored, and bound by the author

Fun in Bluhm

20" x 20" ✳ quilted by the author; colored and pieced with original border design by

Barbara Campbell, Love in Stitches, Pine Brook, New Jersey (www.loveinstitches.com)

Garden to Remember

43" x 43" ✳ *quilted and colored by Gloria West, Fiddlestitch Creek, Holiday, Texas*

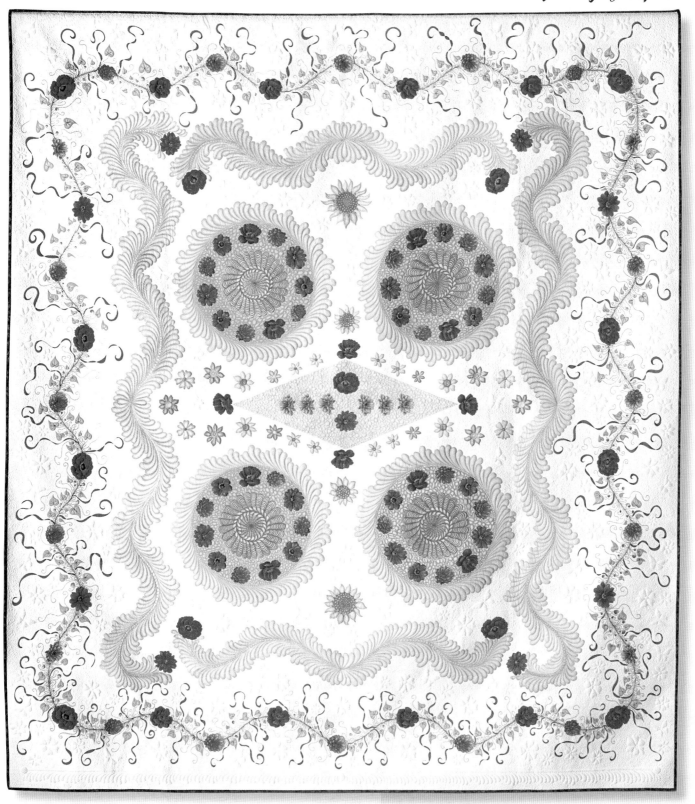

Full Bloom Extravaganza

83" x 95" ✳ quilted and colored by the author

Irena's Sampler

34" x 34" ✱ pattern by the author; quilted by Michelle Miller, Perham, Minnesota

Hummingbird

*89" x 95" * quilted and colored by the author*

Experiment in Color

83" x 95" ✳ *quilted and colored by the author*

Shades of Tiffany

34" x 34" ✳ quilted and colored by Diane L. Anderson, Cabin Quilter Custom Quilting, Tomball, Texas

Butterfly Parade

79" x 85" ✳ *quilted and colored by the author*

Color Me Purple

40" x 40" ✳ *quilted and colored by Cindy Rainey, Kenai, Alaska*

Starburst

52" x 52" ✳ *quilted and colored by the author*

Bluhm Where You Are Planted

54" x 54" ✳ quilted and colored by Diane L. Anderson, Cabin Quilter Custom Quilting, Tomball, Texas

Summer in Bluhm

55" x 69" ✳ quilted and colored by Michelle Miller, Perham, Minnesota

Hawaiian Punch

54" x 54" ✳ quilted and colored by the author

Resources

AMERICAN & EFIRD, INC.
24 American Street
Mt. Holly, NC 28120
Phone: 800-438-5868
Fax: 704-827-0974
Web site: **www.amefird.com**
Distributors of threads
(wholesale)

BLICK ART MATERIALS
PO Box 1267
Galesburg, IL 61402-1267
Phone: 800-828-4548
309-343-6181
(international)
Web site: **www.dickblick.com**

CHERI'S CRYSTALS
Cheri Meineke-Johnson
E-mail:
contact@cheriscrystals.com.
Phone: 940-497-6399
Web site: **www.cheriscrystals.com**

COLUMBIA RIVER QUILTING
1920 NE 149th Avenue
Vancouver, WA 98684
Phone: 360-892-2730 (local)
866-436-7474
(toll free)
Web site:
www.columbiariverquilting.com

DHARMA TRADING CO.
1604 Fourth Street
San Rafael, CA 94901
Phone: 415-456-7657
800-542-5227
Fax: 415-456-8747
Web site:
www.dharmatrading.com

GAMMILL QUILTING SYSTEMS
1452 Gibson Street
West Plains, MO 65775
Phone: 417-256-5919
800-659-8224
Fax: 417-256-5757
E-mail: **info@gammill.net**
Web site: **www.gammill.net**

HOBBS BONDED FIBERS
200 So. Commerce Dr.
Waco, TX 76710
Phone: 1-800-433-3357
Fax: 254-772-7238
E-mail:
sales@HobbsBonded Fibers.com
Web site:
www. hobbsbondedfibers.com

JANET'S QUILTING BEE, INC.
1001 Bowen Avenue
Ocean Springs, MS 39564
Phone: 228-818-9560
Fax: 228-818-9561
E-mail:
thequiltingbee@bellsouth.net.
Web site:
www. janetsquiltingbee.net

JO-ANN FABRIC AND CRAFT STORES
555 Darrow Rd.
Hudson, OH 44236
Phone: 1-800-525-4951
Fax: 330-463-6760
Web site: **www.joann.com**

KING'S MEN QUILTING SUPPLY, INC.
2570 North Walnut
Rochester, IL 62563
Phone: 217-498-9460
        888-744-0070
Fax: 217-498-9476
E-mail: **dtaf@aol.com**
Web site:
www. kmquiltingsupply.com

LINDA'S ELECTRIC QUILTERS, LLC
2001 Central Circle, Suite 103
McKinney, TX 75069
Phone: 800-893-2748
Fax: 800-420-4861
E-mail: **sales@lequilters.com**
Web site: **www. lequilters.com**

PAULA PETERSON'S DESIGNS
PO Box 29
Mead, OK 73449
E-mail: **p3quitler@wildblue.net**

CARLA SCOTT
QUILTED FROG
10550 Rose Bud Court
McKinney, TX 75070
Phone: 972-347-2547
Web site: **www. quiltedfrog.com**
A whimsical collection of patterns for quilters and punch needle embroidery enthusiasts

QUILTERS DREAM BATTING
589 Central Drive
Virginia Beach, VA 23454
Phone: 757-463-3264
888-268-8664
Fax: 757-463-3569
800-626-8866
Web site:
www.quiltersdreambatting.com

RJR FABRICS
2203 Dominguez St. K-3
Torrance, CA 90501
Phone: 800-422-5426
Fax: 310-222-8792
Web site: **www. rjrfabrics.com**
Manufacturers of fabrics and finishers of quilter's sateen

STATLER STITCHER
8801 East Columbus Court
Columbia, MO 65201
Phone: 1-866-830-474-3738
        573-474-0320
Fax: 573-474-0315
E-mail: **paul@statlerstitcher.com**
Web site:
www. statlerstitcher.com
Manufacturer of computerized longarm quilting machine add-ons

SUPERIOR THREADS
87 East 2580 South
St. George, UT 84790
Phone: 435-652-1867
        800-499-1777
Fax: 435-652-4047
E-mail:
info@superiorthreads.com
Web site:
www. superiorthreads.com

YLI CORPORATION
1439 Dave Lyle Blvd.
Rock Hill, SC 29730
Phone: 803-985-3100
Fax: 803-985-3106
E-mail: **ylicorp.@ylicorp.com**
Web site: **www. ylicorp.com**

About the Author

Irena Bluhm is an award-winning quilt artist, quilt and quilting pattern designer, and a longarm machine quilter, instructor, and sales representative for Gammill Quilting Machine Company. Born and raised in Poland during the reign of communism, she moved to Germany in 1981 and ten years later moved to the United States, living in California.

Irena's first sewing experience was at age five, when she tried in secret to use her mother's treadle sewing machine after being told not to touch it. Her legs were short and her little arms lacked coordination, but she was determined to find out if she could sew as her mother did. Alas, one touch of the pedal and her secret was out as the only solution to a needle through her finger was to scream for help!

She watched her seamstress mother making clothes for customers and by the age of nine was helping with the hand finishing. At age 17, she bought an electric sewing machine with her very first paycheck. She learned to make her own clothes and moved on to designing and making garments and wedding dresses for others.

Irena's first exposure to quilting came from the Log Cabin-style quilts her mother made with scraps. She tried some piecing of her own, but quilting didn't become a passion until she saw a Gammill longarm quilting machine at a local quilt shop in 2004. Two days later, Irena was stitching pantographs for the shop owner.

A few days later, she heard about Linda V. Taylor and still remembers seeing her work for the first time. After asking herself how it was possible for any one person to be that good at free-motion quilting, she immediately started to wonder if she could do it herself. It took her a few days, but she convinced her husband to buy a quilting machine. She filled the time between placing her order and the machine's delivery by watching Linda's tapes over and over again. The night the machine arrived, Irena never got to bed.

She never had a business plan to justify her purchase but promised to recover some of the cost by working on customers' quilts. Barely a month later, she was amazed to have her friends tell her she was ready to do "heirloom quilting."

Irena noticed improvement with every quilt she did, giving her the confidence she needed to try making a quilt for show. When her first two wholecloth quilts came back from their first show with three ribbons, she decided to create quilts just for shows. Her work has been exhibited in shows across the United States and published in several quilting magazines. She's won numerous awards nationwide. Irena loves what she does and feels very passionate about quiltmaking and design.

After just a little over two years of longarm quilting experience and teaching at multiple venues across the country, Irena became a national sales representative for Gammill Quilting Machine Company. She has designed pattern collections for Statler Stitcher computerized systems with more to be added. She is ready to try making pictorial quilts, dive deeper into quilt design, and experiment with different techniques. For better or worse, she loves to beat her own path.

Irena has two precious daughters and three gorgeous grandchildren. After her husband Richard retired in 2002, they bought a farm in rural Oklahoma where her large studio is located.

Other AQS Books

This is only a small selection of the books available from the American Quilter's Society. AQS books are known worldwide for timely topics, clear writing, beautiful color photos, and accurate illustrations and patterns. The following books are available from your local bookseller, quilt shop, or public library.

Ribbon Treasures from Celia's Garden — *Faye Labanaris*	Love to Machine Appliqué — A Medley of Techniques — *Caroline Price*	Precious Sunbonnet Quilts — *Betty Alderman*
#7610 us$26.95	#7608 us$26.95	#7604 us$24.95
Award-Winning Appliqué Birds — *Pamela Humphries*	A Black & White Garden — *Kay M. Capps Cross*	Delightful Quilts in Bloom — *Mary Ross & Barbara Scheu*
#7494 us$21.95	#7605 us$24.95	#7602 us$26.95
Scallops Sew Easy — *Marie Seroskie*	100 Things You Need to Know If You Own a Quilt — A Quilt Owner's Manual — *Ann Hazelwood*	Wholecloth Linen Quilts — Patterns & Designs — *Cindy Needham*
#7486 us$22.95	#7558 us$12.95	#7485 us$24.95

Look for these books nationally.
Call or **Visit** our Web site at

1-800-626-5420
www.AmericanQuilter.com